BATTLEFIELDS
in FOCUS

HALLOWED GROUND THROUGH THE CAMERA LENS

by Garry Adelman & Bob Zeller

AMERICAN BATTLEFIELD TRUST ★ ★ ★

PRESERVE. EDUCATE. INSPIRE.

Valley of Death
Gettysburg, Pa.
GARRY ADELMAN

Knox Press
www.KnoxPress.com

First Edition, First Printing © 2024 by American Battlefield Trust
Washington, D.C.

PRINTED IN THE UNITED STATES
Design by Jeff Griffith Creative
Photo editing by Garry Adelman, Chief Historian of the American Battlefield Trust
and Bob Zeller, President of the Center for Civil War Photography
Text by Bob Zeller
Maps by Steven Stanley

Library of Congress Control Number: 2024921979
ISBN: 978-0-9988112-7-7
Published by Knox Press, Princeton, New Jersey

The paper in this book meets the guidelines for performance the durability of the Committee on
Production Guidelines for Book Longevity of the Council on Library Resources.

Cover Photos of Reel Farm by Alexander Gardner / Library of Congress and Matt Brant

TABLE *of* CONTENTS

MESSAGE FROM THE PRESIDENT

DEAR MEMBERS:

60,000 acres.

Our work at the American Battlefield Trust ultimately boils down to a single number — the total acreage of hallowed ground we have preserved since the modern battlefield preservation movement began 37 years ago.

By the time you read these words, this ever-growing number will have already increased. Week by week, month by month, year by year, we make new acquisitions and close deals with willing sellers to preserve their battlefield property.

Since we saved our first 8.55 acres at the Port Republic battlefield in 1988, our reach has expanded to a staggering 160 battlefields in 25 states and has been widened to include the battlefields of the Revolutionary War and the War of 1812.

But what the numbers can't show is the history that has been saved through preservation. An authentic sense of place — the land as it was — has been frozen in time. You can stand at Lee's Head-quarters on Seminary Ridge at Gettysburg and imagine the fury of the fighting during the Battle of Gettysburg. You can now experience the Antietam battlefield as never before, minus several modern buildings the Trust removed from land we were able to purchase with your help.

Dunker Church, 1971,
Antietam National Battlefield
Sharpsburg, Md.
NATIONAL PARK SERVICE

The numbers also don't begin to show the many other bene-fits of battlefield preservation. As we've proven time and again, a preserved battlefield is an economic enginer, driving much-needed tourism dollars to those communities where history was made. Our mission also serves to preserve rapidly disappearing green space. Land marked by combat so many generations ago has been restored by us — whenever possible — to its natural state, providing havens for study, reverie and relaxation.

Battlefields in Focus gives us the opportunity to go beyond the numbers and provide, in a single volume, a showcase of battlefield photography that underscores not only the benefits of battlefield land preservation, but the history and the natural beauty that is saved along with it.

I was at the Antietam battlefield again recently, and was reminded anew of how striking the scene is near the Dunker Church. I was compelled to take yet another photograph from the same spot photographer Alexander Gardner took his famous photo in 1862. As this rarely seen photo above shows, the view wasn't nearly so compelling in 1971, before the National Park Service acquired the land next to the church.

As we prepared this book, I was surprised to see how many Civil War pho-tographs were taken on land or depict land that has been preserved by the Trust and its partners, among them Mathew Brady's iconic photograph of three Rebel prisoners at Gettysburg. The modern pictures, taken by our corps of talented volunteer photographers, display the natural beauty of the land we've saved. This is our legacy as captured in historic and modern photographs.

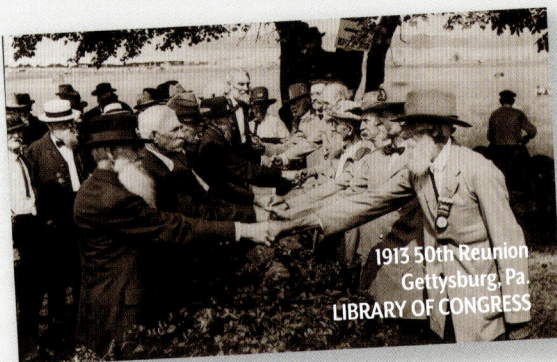

1913 50th Reunion
Gettysburg, Pa,
LIBRARY OF CONGRESS

I am reminded of an image taken at Gettysburg in 1913 at the 50th battle anniversary. Former enemies, now aged men, stand on either side of the Stone Wall at Cemetery Ridge and reach across the divide to shake hands. It exemplifies my conviction that no matter how large our differences are, as Americans we can and should strive for some measure of reconciliation to move our nation forward. For four years, these men had tried to kill each other — and did so with horrible proficiency. But somehow, they found a way to reconcile and live together for the good of our country, always working toward that more perfect union. This is just one of the inspiring lessons from those thousands of preserved acres that we all should take to heart.

David N. Duncan
President, AMERICAN BATTLEFIELD TRUST

INTRODUCTION

SOME OF THE GREATEST PHOTOGRAPHS of the Civil War were taken on battlefield land saved by the American Battlefield Trust.

At Gettysburg, Mathew Brady and his team photographed Lee's Headquarters, which was saved by the Trust in 2015 and restored to its wartime appearance, with the photographs playing a consulting role.

Brady took one of the war's most famous photographs — three Rebel prisoners on Seminary Ridge — on land that has been acquired and preserved by the Trust.

At Antietam, Alexander Gardner took one of his most compelling photographs of the dead Confederates on the battlefield on land the Trust acquired and preserved. Gardner also photographed the ruins of the Reel Barn, as shown on the cover. The Trust has saved that location as well.

From 1987, when the modern battlefield preservation movement began, to 2024, the Trust has saved more than 60,000 acres at more than 160 battlefields of the Civil War, the Revolutionary War and the War of 1812. These acquisitions encompass so many important battlefield locations that they frequently aling with the past at places where Civil War photographs were taken.

In the following pages, as you view both wartime and modern photographs of battlefields and land the Trust has saved, we will cover more than 60 battlefields in 10 states where more than 31,600 acres have been acquired or preserved in more than 500 separate transactions.

But the true scope of the Trust's work and its amazing reach is reflected in dramatic fashion by what goes unmentioned here — what we were forced to leave on the proverbial cutting room floor. Fifteen other states where the Trust has saved Civil War battlefield land must go unmentioned here, along with more than 250 transactions in which we have saved more than 22,300 acres. In Virginia alone, despite all we cover, we had to skip 20 battlefields where we have saved more than 8,200 acres. In most acquisitions, the Trust has partners, especially the federal American Battlefield Protection Program, but often state agencies and local preservation groups as well.

As you read this, the numbers have already grown. Every year, the Trust routinely exceeds a dozen acquisitions and often more than two dozen. In 2023 alone, the Trust closed on 48 different properties at 25 Civil War battlefields and three Revolutionary War battlefields.

The Trust has saved so much at so many different places that it has become common to preserve land where photographs of the Civil War were taken. In fact, it happens so frequently that we decided it was high time that we published a book linking Trust battlefield acquisitions to the photography of the Civil War. In doing so, we hope to underscore in a new and different way the importance of the Trust's land preservation mission and how those vintage photos — literally windows into the past — allow us to see the results of our mission through the lens of history.

CHARLESTON HARBOR

SOUTH CAROLINA

AT 4:30 A.M. on April 12, 1861, after months of tension and controversy over the stubborn federal occupation of Fort Sumter in Charleston Harbor, a Confederate gun at Fort Johnson on James Island fired an exploding shell over the bastion, signaling the start of the bombardment that began the Civil War. Forty-three Confederate cannons arrayed around the harbor opened fire on the fort and its garrison of 85 Union soldiers under the command of Maj. Robert Anderson. They returned fire with some of Sumter's guns but after 34 hours of steady Southern shelling, Anderson surrendered. No one was killed in the bombardment but the war that followed took more than 600,000 lives. The Confederacy managed to hold this fort during the war despite repeated shelling that reduced most of it to rubble. The southern defenders finally abandoned it in February 1865 in the face of Union Gen. William Tecumseh Sherman's advance through South Carolina.

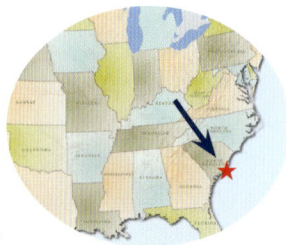

PRESERVATION: In 2008, the Trust and its partners completed one of the epic acquisitions of the modern battlefield preservation movement when they purchased a 117-acre tract on the northern end of Morris Island. The move thwarted two different developers in their plans to build on the uninhabited and undeveloped barrier island. One became so frustrated by the opposition and roadblocks that he offered the property for sale on eBay for $12.5 million before selling it to another developer, who eventually decided to let preservationists buy it for $4.5 million. The island was the site of the Battle of Fort Wagner, made famous by the movie *Glory*. Cummings Point at the northern tip, which was part of the acquisition, was the site of Confederate batteries during the 1861 bombardment, including the Trapier Mortar Battery. This preservation triumph keeps Morris Island as a wild, undeveloped barrier island — a rarity along this coast.

This image of the Trapier Mortar Battery on Morris Island, saved by the American Battlefield Trust and its partners, is one of the first photos of the Civil War. It was taken by Charleston photographers Osborn & Durbec just days after the April 1861 bombardment. ROBIN STANFORD COLLECTION, LIBRARY OF CONGRESS

In one of history's first wartime action photographs, northern photographers Philip Haas and Washington Peale captured the USS *New Ironsides* in combat in Charleston Harbor. Battle smoke rises from the vessel while dozens of Union soldiers watch the fight. It was taken on the beach at the northern end of Morris Island, which has been saved by the Trust and its partners. LIBRARY OF CONGRESS

Morris Island
Charleston, S.C.
BOB ZELLER

RIGHT:
Fort Sumter's exterior as seen from the Stone Wharf in April 1861.
ROBIN STANFORD COLLECTION, LIBRARY OF CONGRESS

BELOW: The interior showing the United States flag-raising ceremony in April 1865. Fort Sumter's hero, Major Robert Anderson. now a general, is visible in uniform in the detail.
LIBRARY OF CONGRESS

Fort Moultrie, 1865
LIBRARY OF CONGRESS

TOP: In August 1860, eight months before the war, Charleston photographers Osborn & Durbec took this photo of the raising of the American flag at neat and trim Fort Moultrie. In the distance on the right looms mighty Fort Sumter with sunlight gleaming off the barracks roofs. BELOW: The modern photo was taken from approximately the same spot in 2017. ROBIN STANFORD COLLECTION, LIBRARY OF CONGRESS; BOB ZELLER.

BULL RUN

VIRGINIA

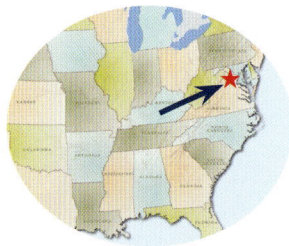

THREE MONTHS after the bombardment of Fort Sumter, a Union Army brimming with confidence marched into Virginia with the aim of capturing Richmond and ending the war. It was confronted near Manassas by a determined Confederate army and fought the first full-scale battle of the Civil War on July 21, 1861. Early in the fight, Union troops forced the Confederates to fall back to Henry House Hill, where Gen. Thomas "Stonewall" Jackson stood "like a stone wall" as the tide of battle turned in favor of the Southerners. As Confederate reinforcements joined the fray, Union setbacks became a rout. As the army fled, civilians who had come to watch the battle joined the panicked flight. More than 60,000 soldiers fought in the battle and more than 4,800 fell, but the staggering toll paled in the face of what was to come. Bull Run ultimately ranked only 30th in the war's bloodiest battles.

PRESERVATION: The Trust has saved 385 acres in 15 acquisitions at the Manassas battlefields, including land on Matthews Hill, where the battle opened with a successful Union advance, and just to the north in the area of Sudley Church and Sudley Springs, where Union troops filled their canteens as they marched onto what became the battlefield.

In March 1862, eight months after the Battle of First Bull Run, when the Union Army first occupied the area, Mathew Brady's photographers George Barnard and James Gibson took this panoramic photo of Henry House Hill. The ruins of the home are visible in the distance at upper right.
LIBRARY OF CONGRESS

A modern image shows the National Park Service visitor center at left center and the reconstructed Henry House at right.
GARRY ADELMAN

Local children face off against seven Union cavalrymen at Catharpin Run near Sudley Church in March 1862. LIBRARY OF CONGRESS

The modern photo below was taken from preserved land, looking across the stream at private property. GARRY ADELMAN

ABOVE: Union graves near Sudley Church (on the hill) and BELOW the scene today. LIBRARY OF CONGRESS; GARRY ADELMAN

Manassas National Battlefield Park
Manassas, Va.
SHENANDOAH SANCHEZ

THE PENINSULA & THE SEVEN DAYS

VIRGINIA

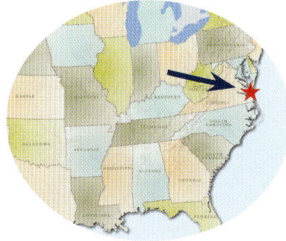

RICHMOND WAS THE TARGET once again as Union Gen. George McClellan led more than 100,000 soldiers of the Army of the Potomac to the Virginia Peninsula in March 1862 and advanced northwest toward the Confederate capital. The Union army gained early success, reaching the outskirts of Richmond by the end of May after fighting at Lee's Mill, a month-long siege at Yorktown and an indecisive battle at Williamsburg. A Confederate surprise attack on May 31 led to the inconclusive battle of Seven Pines, but inflicted more than twice as many casualties as First Bull Run. Confederate Gen. Joseph Johnston was wounded in the battle and replaced by Gen. Robert E. Lee, who aggressively went on the attack in what became the Seven Days Battles, ending the Union campaign and prompting McClellan to retreat, ultimately all the way back to Washington.

PRESERVATION: Very little of the battlefields of the Peninsula Campaign had been saved when the American Battlefield Trust (then the Association for the Preservation of Civil War Sites) made its first acquisition on the Peninsula in 1994, purchasing 518 acres of core battlefield at Malvern Hill, the last of the Seven Days Battles. Since then, the Trust and its partners have acquired an additional 923 acres at Malvern Hill in six transactions as well as more than 1,400 acres at six other Peninsula battlefields, including 363 acres in 11 acquisitions at Gaines' Mill, 710 acres in 18 transactions at Glendale, 343 acres in five transactions at Williamsburg, 11.9 acres at Seven Pines and 5.8 acres at Lee's Mill.

ABOVE: Union Gen. Philip Kearny leads a charge in the Battle of Williamsburg in this sketch by *Harper's Weekly* artist Alfred R. Waud. The modern photo of the battlefield, at right, shows earthworks on land saved by the Trust. LIBRARY OF CONGRESS ; ROBERT JAMES

Land saved by the Trust on Seven Pines Battlefield, Henrico County, Va.
GARRY ADELMAN

BELOW: This expansive photograph by Brady photographer George Barnard shows the Seven Pines battlefield as it looked in June 1862. Today, this is a lost part of the battlefield, with homes and buildings covering this area.
LIBRARY OF CONGRESS

RIGHT: This photo of Prof. Thaddeus Lowe's hydrogen gas balloon *Intrepid* was taken on land saved at Gaines' Mill by the Trust and its partners. LIBRARY OF CONGRESS

BELOW LEFT: An 1865 photo shows unburied dead on the 1862 battlefield at Gaines' Mill before the remains were removed and re-interred. LIBRARY OF CONGRESS

BELOW RIGHT: Modern photo of Cold Harbor National Cemetery. JENNIFER MICHAEL

LEFT: An original hand-colored James Gibson photograph shows the bloody scene at a makeshift field hospital of the 16th New York Infantry at Savage Station after the battle of Gaines' Mill on June 27, 1862. Two days later, most of these men were captured when the armies fought at Savage Station.
LIBRARY OF CONGRESS

The field hospital at Savage Station is now home to a solar farm, an interstate highway and other development.
MARC RAMSEY

SAVAGE STATION
IN THE FIELD BEYOND THIS MARKER WAS
FOUGHT JUNE 29, 1862, THE BATTLE OF SAVAGE STATION
IN WHICH CONFEDERATE FORCES UNDER COMMAND OF

Glendale Battlefield
Richmond National Battlefield Park
Henrico County, Va.
JENNIFER MICHAEL

TOP: Union artillery on Malvern Hill did much to repel one Confederate attack after another in the battle of July 1, 1862. Despite winning this final clash in the Seven Days Battles, the Union Army of the Potomac withdrew and called a halt to the Peninsula Campaign. Much of the battlefield land in this painting and the photo below was saved by the Trust and its partners. NATIONAL PARK SERVICE; JENNIFER GOELLNITZ

SHILOH

TENNESSEE

AS McCLELLAN LAUNCHED the Peninsula Campaign, Gen. U.S. Grant's Union Army was on the move in the Western Theater, marching south along the Tennessee River toward Mississippi. The army was encamped at Pittsburg Landing when the Confederate army under Gen. Albert Sidney Johnston, based in nearby Corinth, Miss., launched a surprise attack on April 6, 1862, and pushed the Yankees back. Union reinforcements arrived and Grant counterattacked the next day, forcing the Confederates to retreat. The bloody battle inflicted more than 23,700 casualties, with each army losing more than 1,700 killed in action. This was the bloodiest battle in American history up to that time.

PRESERVATION: The American Battlefield Trust has been particularly active at Shiloh, acquiring areas of core battlefield that are not already part of the Shiloh National Military Park. Since 2001, the Trust and its partners have acquired more than 1,550 acres in 31 different land transactions ranging from a half-acre to more than 500 acres. Much of this land has been sold or conveyed to the National Park Service.

These Union siege guns of Madison's Battery of the Illinois 2nd Light Artillery were part of Gen. U.S. Grant's "last line" of defense to hold Pittsburg Landing in the Battle of Shiloh. The Trust has preserved several tracts in this area. CIVILWARTALK ONLINE FORUM.

VIEW OF OUR TRANSPORTS AT PITTSBURG LANDING TENN.
APRIL 2ᴰ 1862.

ABOVE: One of three known wartime photos taken at Shiloh, this vintage print of Union steamboats at Pittsburg Landing is labeled April 2, 1862, but is thought to have been taken a few days after the April 6–7 battle. COURTESY FLEISCHER'S AUCTIONS; BELOW: Today, the course of the river is further from the camera. GARRY ADELMAN.

CEDAR MOUNTAIN

VIRGINIA

AFTER **McCLELLAN'S** Peninsula Campaign failed, Gen. John Pope took command of a new Union force, the Army of Virginia, and occupied Northern Virginia. In early August, Pope marched southwest with the aim of capturing the railroad junction at Gordonsville. He never came close. With the threat to Richmond having ended after the Seven Days battles, Lee sent Stonewall Jackson and his corps to Gordonsville to counter Pope's advance. Elements of the two armies clashed at Cedar Mountain, just south of Culpeper, on August 9, 1862. The Union troops nearly drove the Confederates from the field early in the battle, but a counterattack by Confederate Gen. A.P. Hill's division repulsed the Yankees. The Battle of Cedar Mountain gave the Confederates another victory as the fighting in the East moved back to Northern Virginia and Lee gained the upper hand. Almost 25,000 troops were engaged in the battle, which produced some 3,700 casualties.

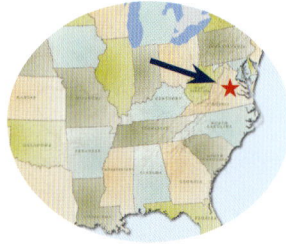

PRESERVATION: The American Battlefield Trust and its partners have acquired and preserved 637 acres in eight transactions as of mid-2024. In 1998, the Trust saved 152 acres of a wheatfield on the battlefield where some of the bloodiest fighting took place. It saved five acres in 2012 just east of the place where Confederate Gen. Charles Winder was mortally wounded. The Cedar Mountain Battlefield Foundation proved instrumental to implementing these preservation efforts and helps to maintain the interpretive trail there. In 2024, the preserved battlefield land at Cedar Mountain became part of the new Culpeper Battlefields State Park.

The Battle of Cedar Mountain was fought near this crossing on August 9, 1862. The back of the photographer's wagon is seen at right. LIBRARY OF CONGRESS

ABOVE: With Cedar Mountain looming in the background, battlefield visitors look at hastily dug Union graves along the Culpeper Road. The Trust has saved this land and leases it for farming. LIBRARY OF CONGRESS. BELOW: GARRY ADELMAN

RIGHT: Furious fighting swept through this scene. All of this land is now preserved by the Trust and its partners. LIBRARY OF CONGRESS

BELOW: After saving the battlefield land shown here, the Trust installed interpretive signage telling the story of the fighting in this field. The road in the vintage photo is on the left of the modern image.

Cedar Mountain Battlefield
Culpeper County, Va.
MATTHEW HARTWIG

Cedar Mountain battlefield after the battle of August 9, 1862. The Trust has saved all this land.
LIBRARY OF CONGRESS

BELOW:
An unidentified family of the battlefield poses outside their home in the wake of the fighting.
LIBRARY OF CONGRESS

SECOND MANASSAS

VIRGINIA

AFTER THE BATTLE of Cedar Mountain, Pope withdrew his army to the Rappahannock River as some Union regiments from McClellan's failed Peninsula Campaign began to arrive to bolster the Army of Virginia. On Aug. 25, 1862, Lee responded by sending Gen. Stonewall Jackson and half the Confederate Army on a wide flanking march to reach Pope's rear and capture the Orange and Alexandria Railroad, cutting off his line of communication and supply. As Pope retreated from the Rappahannock River to respond to the threat, Jackson captured Manassas Junction on August 27, 1862, and destroyed the massive Union supply depot there. Jackson then moved slightly north and occupied a strong defensive position on a stoney ridge along an unfinished railroad cut beside Warrenton Turnpike just west of the First Bull Run battlefield. On August 28, Jackson's "Stonewall Brigade" attacked a Union column passing on the turnpike, triggering a fierce battle that ended in a stalemate. The following day, a massive Union frontal assault failed to dislodge the Confederates in the railroad cut.

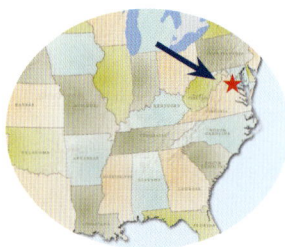

Then, on August 30, as Pope resumed his attack on Jackson's forces, Confederate Gen. James Longstreet crushed the barely-existent Union left, pushing the bluecoats all the way back to Henry House Hill. Jackson repulsed the Union attack on his position and then drove back the Union right. It was another crushing Union defeat and far bloodier than First Bull Run, chalking up more than 14,000 Union casualties and almost 7,400 Confederates. President Lincoln fired Pope on Sept. 2, restored McClellan to full command and ordered him to reorganize the two federal armies into one. Lee, flush with victory, headed north.

PRESERVATION: The American Battlefield Trust and its partners have preserved more than 385 acres on the Manassas battlefields in 15 transactions since 2000. Most of these are on the Second Manassas Battlefield, including parcels of core battlefield land in front of Jackson's line on the unfinished railroad cut and in the area of Longstreet's attack.

An 1880s photograph shows Stonewall Jackson's position north of the Warrenton Turnpike during the Battle of Second Manassas. The Trust has saved land in this area. PRIVATE COLLECTION

ABOVE: One of the first monuments placed on a Civil War battlefield was this one on the Second Manassas battlefield at Groveton, dedicated on June 10, 1865. BELOW: It still stands today minus its adornments. The Trust has preserved several acres in the left distance. LIBRARY OF CONGRESS ; BELOW: GARRY ADELMAN

HARPERS FERRY & SOUTH MTN.

WEST VIRGINIA / MARYLAND

AS McCLELLAN SWIFTLY reorganized Union forces into an 87,000-man Army of the Potomac, Lee invaded the North. The 55,000 soldiers in Lee's Army of Northern Virginia began crossing the Potomac River on Sept. 4 and occupied Frederick, Maryland, on Sept. 6. The following day, McClellan began slowly moving to respond to a threat that sent shock waves through the northern states. Lee divided his army into three parts, sent Jackson to capture Harpers Ferry, Virginia (now West Virginia), and began moving further north. By Sept. 12, McClellan was in Frederick. There, two Union soldiers found three cigars wrapped in a copy of Lee's campaign plan. The famous "lost order" gave McClellan a major advantage in the unfolding campaign. Moving slightly faster, McClellan attacked the three lightly defended passes on South Mountain just west of Frederick on Sept. 14 and pushed the Confederates off the mountain. The following day, Jackson shelled the Union force in Harpers Ferry from the heights above the city and simultaneously launched an infantry attack at Bolivar Heights west of the city. The Union commander, Col. Dixon S. Miles, surrendered his entire force of some 14,000 men. But before he could fly the white flag, Miles was severely wounded in the leg by an exploding shell and died a captive the following day.

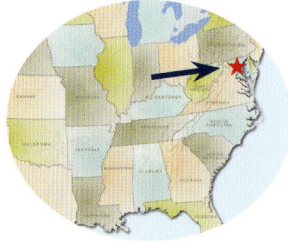

PRESERVATION: The American Battlefield Trust has been particularly active acquiring and preserving land at all of the battlefields of the Maryland Campaign, including South Mountain and Harpers Ferry. In 15 separate transactions since 1991, the Trust has saved 703 acres at South Mountain. This includes key core battlefield land at all three mountain passes where the battle was fought — Turner's Gap, Fox's Gap and Crampton's Gap. The Trust has also been extremely active at previously unprotected Bolivar Heights at Harpers Ferry, where Jackson launched his infantry attack on Sept. 15. In nine transactions from 1992 through mid-2024, the Trust saved 542 acres at the Harpers Ferry battlefield.

This 1859 photo shows the engine house at left and the arsenal after John Brown's Raid and much as it looked when war broke out in 1861.
HARPERS FERRY NATIONAL HISTORIC PARK

ABOVE: Harpers Ferry sits at the confluence of the Potomac River (right) and the Shenandoah River (left). SHENANDOAH SANCHEZ

LEFT: The town was photographed many times during the war, including this photo that shows the ruins of the railroad bridge whose piers still stand today. LIBRARY OF CONGRESS.

Mathew Brady and his team photographed the 22nd New York Infantry Regiment at Harpers Ferry in the summer of 1862. The Trust and its partners have saved substantial acreage to the left of this photo in an area that would see Stonewall Jackson's forces defeat the Union Army in the Battle of Harpers Ferry on Sept. 12-15, 1862. NATIONAL ARCHIVES

This lithograph engraving shows the Union assault on Fox's Gap during the Battle of South Mountain on Sept. 14, 1862, from a bird's-eye perspective. Much of the land visible in the lithograph has been saved by the Trust or other organizations. LIBRARY OF CONGRESS

South Mountain
Middletown, Md.
ROBERT FOX

This post-war photograph shows the Wise house, which was near the highest point at Fox's Gap and close to where Union Gen. Jesse Reno was mortally wounded. Most of the land around the gap has been preserved by the Trust and other preservation organizations.
BOB ZELLER COLLECTION

Fox's Gap
South Mountain State Battlefield
Middletown, Md.
NOEL KLINE

ANTIETAM

MARYLAND

LEE WAS DETERMINED to make a stand in Maryland, hoping to crush the Union Army on its own soil. He began consolidating his scattered forces on high ground along Antietam Creek just outside Sharpsburg, Maryland. McClellan advanced cautiously and took an extra day, Sept. 16, 1862, to perfect his battle plans. "It was now evident that the morrow would be a day of blood," wrote a Confederate artillerist. McClellan's troops attacked piecemeal — first Hooker's troops at the Cornfield followed by Gen. Edwin Sumner's Corps into the hellish West Woods and at the Sunken Road and finally Burnside's struggle to cross the bridge over Antietam Creek that now bears his name. Burnside's advance might have won the day but for a final Confederate arrival from Harpers Ferry — Gen. A.P. Hill's 3,000-man division — that stopped his troops cold. It was the bloodiest single day of the war and, indeed, September 17, 1862, still stands as the bloodiest day in American history, with more than 22,700 casualties. Lee remained at Sharpsburg for a desultory extra day, but withdrew back into Virginia on Sept. 19, repulsing the pursuing Union troops in the Battle of Shepherdstown and driving them back across the Potomac. The fighting at Antietam had been inconclusive, but Lee's withdrawal gave President Lincoln enough of a victory to announce the Emancipation Proclamation on Sept. 22.

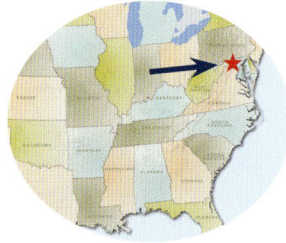

PRESERVATION: The original Antietam National Battlefield was established in 1890 as a low-budget endeavor, with only enough land purchases to establish rights of way for a coach or driving tour. In the years since, much of the battlefield has been purchased and added to the battlefield park, but even today core battlefield land remains in private hands. The Trust, however, has done much to change that since its first acquisition at Antietam in 1991, preserving 488 acres in 13 separate transactions. One of the biggest saves in the Trust's history was its 2015 purchase of the triangular 44-acre "epicenter" tract of core battlefield land along Hagerstown Pike between the Cornfield and the Dunker Church. Since 2004, the Trust and its partners also have made 14 saves at Shepherdstown, preserving a total of 893 acres of that battlefield.

The body of a young Confederate soldier lies unburied next to the grave of Lt. John C. Clark of the 7th Michigan in the "epicenter" tract in the heart of the Antietam battlefield, which has been preserved by the Trust.
LIBRARY OF CONGRESS

LEFT: Confederates from Louisiana were photographed as they fell along Hagerstown Pike during furious fighting at Antietam. The land where the wagons are parked has been saved by the Trust.
LIBRARY OF CONGRESS

BELOW: The dead Confederates photographed by Alexander Gardner along Hagerstown Pike are morphed into a modern image in this photo illustration.
LARRY KASPEREK

Entered according to the Act of Congress, in the year 1862, by ALEX. GARDNER, in the Clerk's Office of the District Court of the District of Columbia.

ABOVE: In this hand-colored Alexander Gardner stereo view, three Union soldiers and a civilian pose next to some of Antietam's dead on Sept. 20, 1862, three days after the battle. BELOW: Photohistorian William A. Frassanito found the distinctive limestone outcropping seen in both photos along the south side of Cornfield Avenue. Edward Richter poses in the modern photo taken in 2012. BOB ZELLER

ABOVE: The barn on David Reel's farm just behind Confederate battle lines at Antietam was filled with wounded Rebels when it was set afire by a Union shell, trapping some of them.
BELOW: The Reel farm saved by the Trust and the barn has been improved and stablized.
LIBRARY OF CONGRESS; MATT BRANT

ABOVE: Dead Confederate artillerymen lie next to an abandoned limber on the Antietam battlefield in this famous photo taken by Alexander Gardner at about 7:30 a.m. on Sept. 20, 1862, three days after the battle. In the background is the shell-damaged Dunker Church, named for the sect of pacifists who worshiped there, eschewing embellishments such as church steeples. The label on the back of original copies of this photo is at left. The Trust has preserved substantial acreage to the left of and behind the church. LIBRARY OF CONGRESS

In this photo illustration, a modern photo of the inside of the Dunker Church is enhanced with elements of a separate photo showing a Civil War reenactment. LARRY KASPEREK

A wagon crosses Burnside Bridge just days after the battle. The three-arch stone bridge, built in 1836, was a toll bridge during the war and continued to handle regular traffic until 1966. BOB ZELLER COLLECTION.

Westward view of Antietam Battlefield from Red Hill. Keedysville, Md.
LARRY KASPEREK

CORINTH
MISSISSIPPI

ON OCT. 3, 1862, as President Lincoln visited McClellan at the Antietam battlefield, urging him to take the Army of the Potomac into Virginia to pursue Lee, a 22,000-man Confederate army attacked about 23,000 Union troops at Corinth, Mississippi. Union forces had occupied Corinth, a key railroad junction and transportation center in northern Mississippi, after the victory at Shiloh. The federals were driven back toward the city as the Confederates won the day. When the battle resumed the following day, Union troops had regrouped and held several strong redoubts. The Rebels pressed forward through fierce artillery fire and managed to take Battery Powell, but the Yankees held Battery Robinett in desperate hand-to-hand combat, then retook Battery Powell and drove the Confederates back. After two days of combat and more than 7,000 casualties, Union forces won the battle.

PRESERVATION: The American Battlefield Trust has been particularly active at the largely unprotected battlefield at Corinth. Although Battery Robinett is preserved as part of the Shiloh National Military Park, the Trust and its partners have saved 824 acres of the battlefield in 14 separate transactions since 1994.

ABOVE: A three-plate panorama looking generally west with the Tishomingo Hotel and railroad station at left and Batteries Williams and Robinett at center. LIBRARY OF CONGRESS/SHILOH NATIONAL MILITARY PARK. BELOW: GARRY ADELMAN.

LEFT: This recently discovered image of Confederate dead where they fell on a battlefield — the 104th known image of Civil War battlefield dead, may have been taken at Corinth but a positive identification has yet to be made. RON PERISHO COLLECTION.

BELOW: Part of the Corinth battlefield is visible in this scene, which shows the same area as the right side of the vintage panorama on page 40. LIBRARY OF CONGRESS

+ Where Col Rogers 2d Texas Killed Oct-3/62

Scene at Corinth Miss

"Fort Robinett" Corinth Miss.

FREDERICKSBURG

VIRGINIA

O N NOVEMBER 5, 1862, President Lincoln reached the end of his rope with McClellan's inaction and replaced him with a reluctant Gen. Ambrose Burnside, who led the Army of the Potomac toward Richmond. Both armies concentrated their forces at Fredericksburg and on Dec. 11, Union forces battled across the Rappahannock River, engaged Confederate forces in the first urban combat of the Civil War and occupied the city. Two days later, the Army of the Potomac launched an all-out attack on the well-entrenched Confederate line on Marye's Heights, sending brigade after brigade across an open plain toward a stone wall where Confederates were lined three deep. Union troops were mowed down before they ever reached the wall. Two and a half miles to the south, the federals launched a massive attack on Jackson's Confederates and briefly opened a hole in the Confederate line, but Jackson's counterattack beat them back. Some 200,000 men on both sides were engaged in what became one of the Union army's most devastating losses. Burnside's army suffered some 12,500 casualties, more than twice as many as Lee's army, and fell back across the Rappahannock to Falmouth.

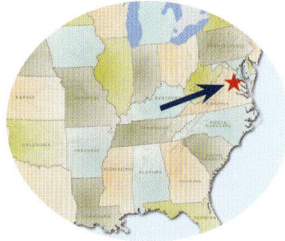

PRESERVATION: One of the American Battlefield Trust's greatest preservation triumphs was the acquisition of the 208-acre Slaughter Pen Farm in the heart of the southern part of the Fredericksburg battlefield. Farm owner John Pierson had resisted eager buyers for years as development spread through the area. A year after his death in 2005, the Trust was able to purchase the tract for $12 million, by far the largest deal in its history. In 2022, it finally paid off the last of the debt it had incurred with the purchase. In seven other transactions, the Trust has preserved an additional 58 acres at Fredericksburg.

This recently identified panoramic photograph provides a remarkable, new view of Fredericksburg under Confederate control in early 1863. Confederate cavalry are visible by the road at upper left, Marye's Heights and the Stone Wall are at upper center and the chimneys of homes that burned during the bombardment in December 1862 are visible at right.
UNIVERSITY OF MARYLAND, BALTIMORE COUNTY

Fredericksburg, Va.
From the north bank of the Rappahannock River.
BUDDY SECOR

ABOVE: Two Brady wartime photographs are combined to create a panorama of Marye's Heights and the bloody battlefield where one Union assault after another was crushed on December, 13, 1862. BELOW: Several of the damaged structures in this photo of Fredericksburg appear at the right edge of the panorama above. NATIONAL ARCHIVES; LIBRARY OF CONGRESS

In this painting by Carl Röchling, the Zouaves of the 114th Pennsylvania under Col. Charles H.T. Collis charge forward in their first taste of combat at Slaughter Pen Farm during the Battle of Fredericksburg. Collis was awarded the Medal of Honor for his leadership in the battle. AMERICAN BATTLEFIELD TRUST

Slaughter Pen Farm
Fredericksburg Battlefield
Fredericksburg, Va.
BUDDY SECOR

CHANCELLORSVILLE / SECOND FREDERICKSBURG

VIRGINIA

BURNSIDE'S FAILURES led President Lincoln to replace him with Gen. Joseph Hooker. After revitalizing the army, Hooker led it across the Rappahannock in late April 1863 and prepared to flank Lee's army at Fredericksburg from the west. Lee recognized the threat and moved most of his army to block Hooker's advance. On May 1, Confederates under Stonewall Jackson stymied the Federal advance. Hooker flinched, surrendered the initiative and pulled his army back to Chancellorsville. The following day, in one of his most daring and dramatic moves, Lee sent Stonewall Jackson's corps of nearly 30,000 men on a 12-mile flanking march around Hooker's army. That evening, they launched a devastating attack on Hooker's flank, sending most of the Union troops fleeing in panic. After nightfall, Jackson rode ahead of his line to scout the enemy and was fatally wounded by his own troops. Following two more days of bloody fighting, Hooker was defeated and retreated back across the Rappahannock on May 5. Four days of intense fighting left more than 30,000 casualties, including more than 17,300 Union soldiers and some 13,460 Confederates.

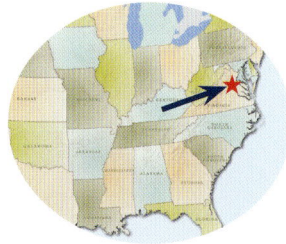

PRESERVATION: The Trust took on one of the most intense battles against development in its history with its opposition to a massive development on the first day's battlefield beginning in 2002. Ultimately, it joined with another developer to acquire the land and in two separate acquisitions in 2004 and 2005, preserved 134 acres of the core battlefield while allowing development on other less historic acreage. Since 2002, in 18 acquisitions, the Trust and its partners have saved 1,338 acres of the Chancellorsville battlefield.

LEFT: Dowdall's Tavern was situated directly in the path of Jackson's flank attack. The site was preserved by the American Battlefield Trust. LIBRARY OF CONGRESS. BELOW: An 1866 photo of the ruins of the Chancellor House, which burned during the battle. LIBRARY OF CONGRESS

This image, taken in 1866, is the earliest known photo showing the place (just inside the woodline where the men are stading) where Confederate Gen. Thomas "Stonewall" Jackson was mortally wounded on May 2, 1863. PRIVATE COLLECTION

An 1880s photo showing the memorial rock placed at the fatal spot. PRIVATE COLLECTION.

BELOW: This stunning panorama shows Fredericksburg at war on May 3, 1863, with battle smoke rising on the left. It was created from several separate photos taken by U.S. Army Capt. A. J. Russell during the so-called Second Battle of Fredericksburg, part of the Battle of Chancellorsville.
LARRY KASPEREK / CENTER FOR CIVIL WAR PHOTOGRAPHY

ABOVE: During the Battle of Chancellorsville, Union soldiers of Brooks's Division of the Sixth Corps occupied abandoned Confederate works on the west bank of the Rappahannock River, ready to launch an assault at a moment's notice. NATIONAL ARCHIVES

RIGHT: This 1866 photo shows the women of the Hawkins family, who witnessed unforgettable sights during the frantic Union retreat in the face of Stonewall Jackson's flank attack on May 2, 1863, during the Battle of Chancellorsville. ROBIN STANFORD COLLECTION, LIBRARY OF CONGRESS

LEFT: Union Gen. Herman Haupt (left) and an assistant view the remains of a wrecked caisson not far from the Stone Wall at Fredericksburg after Union forces took the position in fighting on May 3, 1863, during the Battle of Chancellorsville. LIBRARY OF CONGRESS.

BELOW:
Stone Wall at Marye's Heights. Fredericksburg & Spotsylvania National Military Park. Fredericksburg, Va. MIKE TALPLACIDO

BRANDY STATION
VIRGINIA

ON JUNE 3, 1863, the first elements of Lee's 75,000-man Army of Northern Virginia began marching west out of Fredericksburg. Lee had decided to invade the North once more, and what became the Gettysburg Campaign had begun. By June 9, the army was in Culpeper and the cavalry under Gen. J.E.B. Stuart guarded the Rappahannock near Brandy Station, watching for Union activity. Early that morning, two columns of Union horsemen, supported by infantry crossed the river to attack Stuart's cavalry camp. A sharp, pre-dawn skirmish triggered the greatest cavalry battle ever fought in North America. For 12 hours, almost 20,000 troopers on both sides attacked and counterattacked. Stuart staved off defeat in frantic fighting on Fleetwood Hill. At the end of the day, Confederates held the field, but the Union cavalry had fought well and effectively, boosting their morale after enduring earlier defeats by Stuart's mounted force.

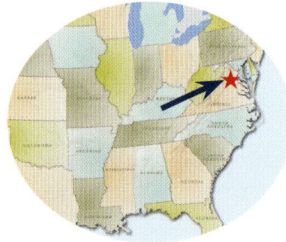

PRESERVATION: The Brandy Station battlefield was entirely unprotected and under private ownership in the late 1980s. As it began to face development threats, the modern battlefield preservation movement got underway with the creation of the Trust's foundational organization, the Association for the Preservation of Civil War Sites (APCWS). One of APCWS's greatest victories was the preservation of almost 700 acres of the battlefield in 1997. Since then, the Trust has steadily added to the amount of battlefield land saved in Brandy Station. After 18 additional transactions, the Trust has now saved 2,252 acres of the battlefield, which in 2024 became, along with Cedar Mountain, the new Culpeper Battlefields State Park.

Hundreds of photos were taken in and around Brandy Station, Va., during the Civil War, including this winter scene on Fleetwood Hill, a strategically crucial prominence in the Battle of Brandy Station that has been saved by the Trust.
PHOTO COURTESY
CLARK "BUD" HALL

ABOVE: Looking east toward Fleetwood Hill, which historian Clark "Bud" Hall describes as "the most marched upon, camped upon, fought upon, fought over piece of real estate in American history." PHOTO COURTESY CLARK "BUD" HALL; BELOW: A watercolor by Robert Knox Sneden shows Fleetwood Hill, with the same tree appearing in both the artwork and the photo. NATIONAL ARCHIVES

A modern photo shows Fleetwood Hill from the same approximate vantage point as the images on page 51. Informational markers installed by the Trust atop the hill lead visitors on one of three interpretive trails at Brandy Station. CLARK "BUD" HALL; JENNIFER MICHAEL

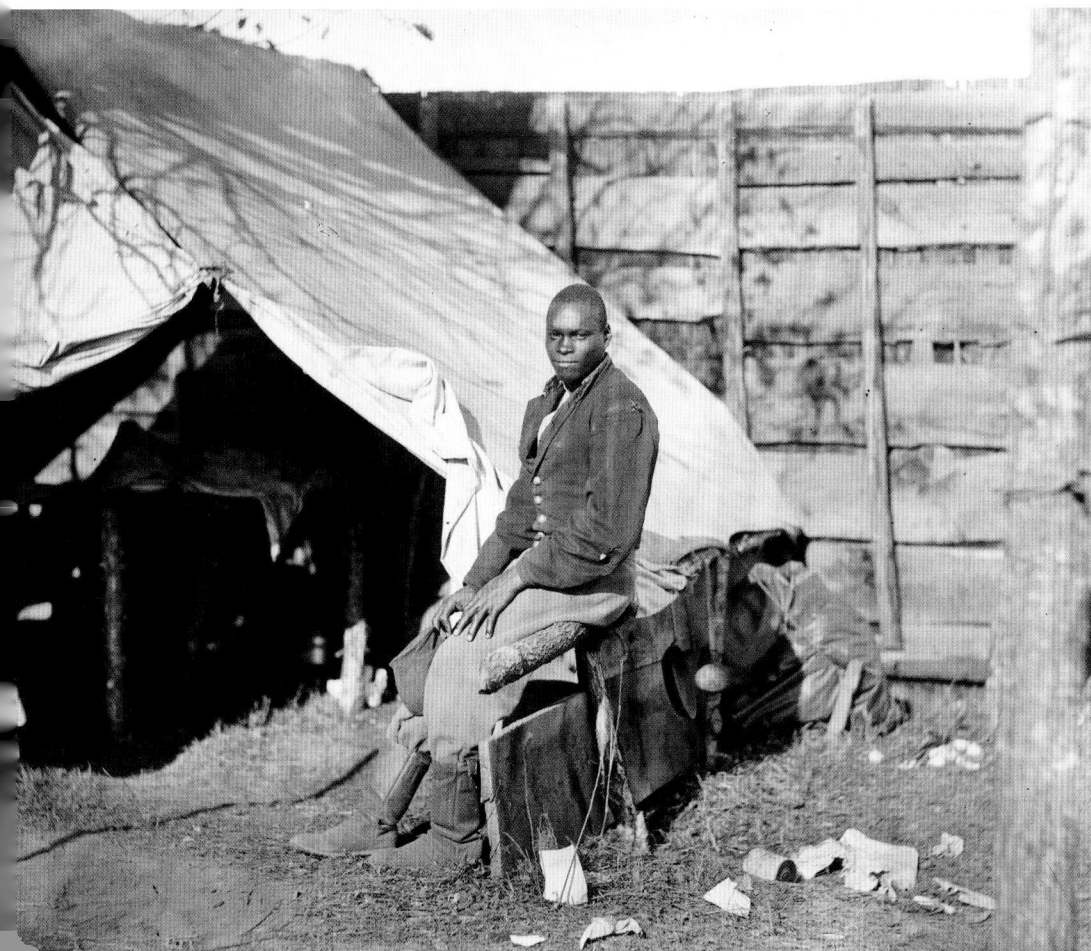

ABOVE: Gen. George Meade poses with Generals Robert Tyler, Alfred Pleasonton, John Sedgwick, Alfred Torbert and others at the Army of the Potomac Horse Artillery headquarters at Brandy Station in February 1864 on land now pre-served by the American Battlefield Trust. LIBRARY OF CONGRESS

LEFT: An unidentified camp servant known then as a "contraband" poses by a tent in a Union camp at Culpeper, Va., in November 1863. BELOW: A closeup taken from the original glass plate negative shows the level of detail visible in many Civil War photos. LIBRARY OF CONGRESS

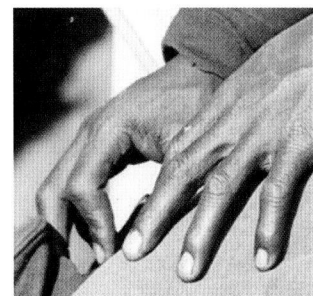

GETTYSBURG
PENNSYLVANIA

A SENSE OF PANIC spread through Pennsylvania and the North in mid-June as Lee's troops began crossing the Potomac once again. Lee was seeking fresh supplies, food and a victory in a battle on Northern soil that might force a negotiated end to the war. Hooker, humbled by Chancellorsville, was indecisive. On June 28, 1863, President Lincoln accepted Hooker's resignation and replaced him with Gen. George Meade, who moved rapidly north to confront Lee. On the morning of July 1, Union cavalry pickets collided with Confederate infantry at Gettysburg. The fighting expanded and grew more intense as both armies began converging there. By the end of the day, the federals had been pushed back through the town but occupied high ground on Culp's Hill, Cemetery Hill and Little Round Top. On July 2, the Confederates launched attacks on the Union left at Little Round Top, Devil's Den, the Wheatfield and the Peach Orchard. On the Union right, the Confederates attacked Culp's Hill and Cemetery Hill. After bitter, heavy fighting, the Union line held. On July 3, following a massive artillery barrage, some 12,500 Confederates marched a mile across an open plain to attack the Union center on Cemetery Ridge. Pickett's Charge ground to a halt in a maelstrom of smoke, musket fire, artillery explosions and hand-to-hand combat. The Confederate survivors, battered and beaten, staggered back across the field in retreat and then back to Virginia as the Union army claimed a decisive victory. It was the bloodiest battle of the Civil War. Of the more than 165,000 soldiers engaged in the fight, more than 51,000 were killed, wounded, captured or missing after the battle.

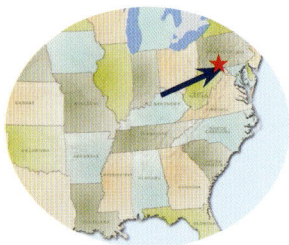

PRESERVATION: When Gettysburg National Military Park was established in 1895, it included some 800 acres near Union lines, such as Culp's Hill and Little Round Top. Confederate lines on Seminary Ridge were not part of the park and remained privately owned. The Widow Thompson house, which was Lee's headquarters, became a private museum and motel/restaurant complex. The Trust, in one of its greatest preservation saves, acquired the 4.14-acre property in 2015, removed the modern buildings, restored the house, created an interpretive walking trail and opened it to the public in 2016. The Trust's preservation record is befitting of the Civil War's greatest battle, with 1,277 acres of battlefield land preserved in 46 different transactions since 1997, and more to come.

The three Confederate captives in the full-frame version of this classic Mathew Brady photograph stand on Seminary Ridge.
GILDER LEHRMAN INSTITUTE OF AMERICAN HISTORY

1863

The Mary Thompson house, where Gen. Robert E. Lee had his headquarters during the Battle of Gettysburg, was preserved by the Trust in 2015 and restored the following year. LIBRARY OF CONGRESS; MIDDLE / BOTTOM: GARRY ADELMAN

2014

2016

The Lutheran Theological Seminary was captured in a Brady photograph in mid-July 1863 (above right), and as it looks today. Also in the photo is the eastern slope of Seminary Ridge, on which the Trust secured an easement in 2019.
LIBRARY OF CONGRESS; GARRY ADELMAN

This spectacular then-and-now pair taken from Little Round Top shows the Valley of Death, the Rose Woods at right and Seminary Ridge in the mid-distance as depicted in a Mathew Brady photograph taken in mid-July 1863 and in a modern photo. Brady himself appears below and to the right of the stone wall in the foreground, wearing a black-banded straw skimmer hat. MOLLUS COLLECTION, U.S. ARMY HERITAGE AND EDUCATION CENTER; GARRY ADELMAN.

The partially buried boulder seen at left in this then-and-now pair became one of the puzzle pieces that fell into place for photohistorian William A. Frassanito, allowing him to determine that Alexander Gardner's series depicting dead in this field were taken on the Rose Farm. LIBRARY OF CONGRESS; GARRY ADELMAN.

The American Battlefield Trust and its partners have been especially active in preserving land associated with the Union right flank at Gettysburg, saving several properties near Powers Hill, which looms above the Baltimore Pike in the upper photo. Its clear slopes proved an ideal platform for Union artillery. At the base of and atop East Cemetery Hill, the Trust has preserved multiple properties including the woods at far left in the photo below.
GETTYSBURG NATIONAL MILITARY PARK; NOEL KLINE

VICKSBURG

MISSISSIPPI

O**N JULY 4, 1863,** the day after Pickett's Charge at Gettysburg, Confederate Gen. John Pemberton surrendered his beleaguered army of some 29,000 men at Vicksburg following a 47-day siege. The Union victory was the culmination of an 18-month campaign by Gen. U.S. Grant, who had doggedly pursued the critical Confederate stronghold on the Mississippi River despite one setback after another. After more than a year of futility, Grant took his army into Louisiana, marched south of Vicksburg and crossed the river into Mississippi on April 30, 1863, the same day Hooker encamped at Chancellorsville on the eve of the battle there. Grant moved swiftly northeast, beating the Southerners at every turn. He captured the state capital at Jackson on May 14, then turned west toward Vicksburg and defeated the Confederates in battles at Raymond, Champion Hill and Big Black River Bridge, forcing them back to Vicksburg. After bloody frontal assaults failed on May 19 and May 22, Grant laid siege to the surrounded city to starve the Confederates and Vicksburg's occupants into submission.

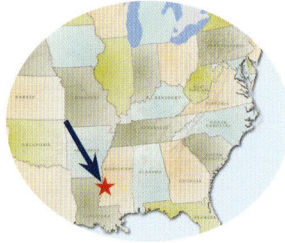

The capture of this vital river city effectively cut the Confederacy in half. The Confederate military would maintain a fearsome fighting force for months to come, but would never recover from the back-to-back defeats at Gettysburg and Vicksburg.

PRESERVATION: The Vicksburg National Battlefield Park was established in 1899 and preserves much of the battlefield and the opposing lines during the siege of the city. However, core battlefield land at the edges of the park remained in private hands, as did all of the battlefields at Raymond, Champion Hill and Big Black River Bridge. Since 2013, the Trust has saved 46 acres at Vicksburg in seven acquisitions and 25 acres at Chickasaw Bayou in 17 transactions. It has preserved 149 acres of the Raymond battlefield and 28 acres at Big Black River Bridge. At crucial Champion Hill, where the Confederates made a stand and lost more than 6,200 men killed, wounded, captured or missing, nothing was preserved until 2003. Since then, the Trust and its partners have saved 1,228 acres in 15 acquisitions.

The mighty Mississippi River flows by Vicksburg, Miss., in this wartime photograph. LIBRARY OF CONGRESS

Here at Chickasaw Bayou, Union Gen. W.T. Sherman's troops failed in their assault on Confederate lines in December 1862 in the opening battle of the Vicksburg Campaign. LIBRARY OF CONGRESS

Chickasaw Bayou Battlefield
Warren County, Miss.
MIKE TALPLACIDO

The Trust has been especially active at Vicksburg Campaign sites, saving the core of the battlefield around the Champion Hill crossroads ABOVE and several properties along the Vicksburg Siege lines shown BELOW. Both: MIKE TALPLACIDO

Soldiers on both sides as well as Vicksburg residents sought shelter ABOVE from heat and artillery shells in caves and makeshift lean-tos built into the bluffs around the river town, including at the Shirley House, which still stands BELOW today. SMITHSONIAN AMERICAN ART MUSEUM; GARRY ADELMAN

PORT HUDSON

LOUISIANA

ON MAY 21, 1863, three days after Grant laid siege on Vicksburg, Union troops also began the siege of Port Hudson, La., a Mississippi River town just north of Baton Rouge. Union assaults on May 27 and June 14 failed to dislodge the Confederates or force them to give up, so the siege continued. When news of the surrender of Vicksburg reached Port Hudson, the last Confederate garrison on the Mississippi River, still barely holding out, realized there was no hope and the force of some 7,000 men surrendered. In Washington, Lincoln said, "Thank God. The Father of Waters again goes unvexed to the sea."

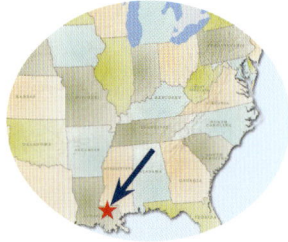

PRESERVATION: In two acquisitions, the Trust has saved more than 258 acres at Port Hudson, allowing the State Park to expand its walking trails and solidify key portions of the battlefield where Black soldiers trained for the fighting to come.

Port Hudson State Historic Site
Jackson, La.
GERARD PLAUCHE

The Confederates who held this fortification throughout the 48-day siege at Port Hudson named it Fort Desperate. The defenders withstood two ferocious Union assaults in some of the most intense fighting at this Mississippi River bastion. The lower photo shows the same perspective at Fort Desperate. ROBIN STANFORD COLLECTION, LIBRARY OF CONGRESS; GARRY ADELMAN.

CHICKAMAUGA
GEORGIA

IN SEPTEMBER 1863, Union Gen. William S. Rosecrans and the Army of the Cumberland began moving on Chattanooga, a key junction of four railroads where the Tennessee River cut through the Cumberland Plateau. It was held by the Confederate Army of Tennessee under Gen. Braxton Bragg, who abandoned the city when he realized the Union Army was crossing Lookout Mountain to his south and flanking him. Rosecrans entered Chattanooga unopposed on Sept. 9, then advanced into Georgia, where Bragg struck back. The battle began on Sept. 18 along a ragged three-mile line near West Chickamauga Creek. Bragg's men launched a series of aggressive assaults that pushed the Union troops back but failed to break their line. That evening, Gen. James Longstreet arrived with reinforcements. Now the Confederates had some 65,000 men, while the Union army had about 60,000. The next day, after more bloody fighting in the morning, Union forces continued to hold until Longstreet attacked at an inadvertent gap in the Union line, sending part of the army,

including Rosecrans, in panicked retreat. Only a small percentage of the army under the leadership of Gen. George H. Thomas fought on, doggedly holding high ground at Snodgrass Hill and Horseshoe Ridge while fighting off desperate Confederate assaults. That evening, Thomas conducted an orderly withdrawal toward Chattanooga. He would soon earn the name "The Rock of Chickamauga" for his brave stand against enormous odds, but the two-day battle was a decisive Confederate victory. It was also the bloodiest battle in the West and the second bloodiest of the entire war, trailing only Gettysburg, with almost 35,000 casualties.

PRESERVATION: Much of the Chickamauga battlefield is preserved as part of the Chickamauga & Chattanooga National Military Park, but as is usually the case, some core battlefield land remains in private hands. Since 2013, the Trust has saved 145 acres at Chickamauga, including the area around Reed's Bridge, where the opening shots of the battle were fired on Sept. 18.

The Battle of Chickamauga began on September 18, 1863, at Reed's Bridge, sketched here by artist Alfred R. Waud. The Trust has preserved land on both sides of the bridge.
LIBRARY OF CONGRESS

Lee and Gordon's Mill on Chickamauga Creek, shown during the Civil War ABOVE and today BELOW. The mill was the site of constant skirmishing during the Battle of Chickamauga. LIBRARY OF CONGRESS; GARRY ADELMAN

CHATTANOOGA

TENNESSEE

THE ARMY OF THE CUMBERLAND fell back to Chattanooga after its defeat at Chickamauga, prompting Confederate Gen. Braxton Bragg to besiege the city. On Oct. 16, 1863, Grant was put in command of all the Union armies in the West and he replaced Rosecrans with Thomas in Chattanooga, ordering four divisions under Gen. William T. Sherman to join him. Soon after, Union troops foiled the siege by establishing a "Cracker Line" across the Tennessee River to keep the army fed as Grant made plans to attack Bragg and break the siege. On Nov. 23, Union troops drove the Confederates from Orchard Knob, an eminence about a mile from the main Confederate line at Missionary Ridge. The following day, Union troops charged up and took Lookout Mountain. And on Nov. 25, a dramatic, direct Union assault up Missionary Ridge shattered the Confederate line and forced Bragg and his army to retreat back into Georgia. The way was now clear for Union troops to advance into Georgia and drive toward Atlanta and the sea. The three-day battle led to about 13,800 casualties, a fearsome toll on its face but not particularly brutal by Civil War standards.

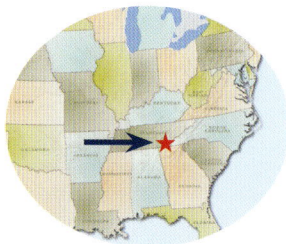

PRESERVATION: In eight acquisitions since 2005, the Trust and its partners have preserved 405 acres at Chattanooga, including a large parcel atop Lookout Mountain and Brown's Ferry on the Tennessee River across from the city, where Union troops broke the month-long Confederate siege and established the "Cracker Line" to resupply the starving Union troops.

In 1866, photographer George Barnard photographed Missionary Ridge at Chattanooga, where Union troops routed the Confederates in one of the war's most famous assaults. THE METROPOLITAN MUSEUM OF ART

ABOVE: Union Gen. U.S. Grant appears with others in this 1864 photograph at Roper's Rock on Lookout Mountain. In 2011, BELOW, Trust department heads (from left) Garry Adelman, Tom Gilmore and Jim Campi posed in the same place. ANTHONY HODGES COLLECTION; ROB SHENK.

This then-and-now pair shows Orchard Knob and Missionary Ridge in the distance as photographed by George Barnard in 1866 and captured through the lens of a digital camera in 2011. Gen. U. S. Grant watched from here as his Union troops charged up the steep ridge and routed the Confederates in one of the war's most famous assaults.
METROPOLITAN MUSEUM OF ART; GARRY ADELMAN

BELOW: After saving battlefield land, the Trust often removes any non-historic structures, as it did at this preserved parcel on the battlefield of Lookout Mountain.
LEFT: BRIAN KEELEY PHOTOGRAPHY; RIGHT: ANTHONY HODGES.

ABOVE: It's almost certain that more photographs were taken during the Civil War here at Point Lookout on Lookout Mountain than any other location. In the vintage photo, photographer Royan Linn (right) poses with two assistants and a stereo camera.
BELOW: Wet plate photographer Wendell Decker is shown posing Rebecca David and Jeffrey David during the 2011 Image of War seminar conducted by The Center for Civil War Photography. ANTHONY HODGES COLLECTION; BOB ZELLER.

SHENANDOAH VALLEY

VIRGINIA

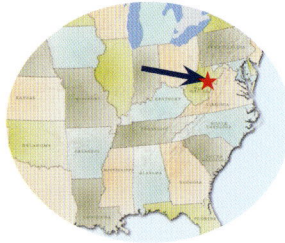

THE 150-MILE-LONG Shenandoah Valley of Virginia was one of the most crucial geographic features of the Civil War for both sides. Strategically, the Blue Ridge mountains, on the east side of the valley, provided backdoor routes to both Washington, D. C. and Richmond. But it was far more crucial to the South as a breadbasket of wheat, grains and produce for the Confederacy and the Army of Northern Virginia. It also carried symbolic importance, "an iconic Confederate place," as one scholar describes it. During his Valley Campaign of 1862, Gen. Stonewall Jackson exploited the 'home turf' to foil the Union army at almost every turn and help stall the Union efforts to capture Richmond. The Confederates used the Valley to invade the north in 1863 and threaten Washington in 1864. Finally, in his Shenandoah Campaign of 1864. Union Gen. Philip Sheridan defeated the Confederates in the bloody battles of Third Winchester, Fisher's Hill and Cedar Creek while conducting a scorched earth campaign that drove a stake in the Valley's ability to provide sustenance to the South. Winchester, the largest city in the northern Valley, was the most contested city of the war, changing hands some 70 times.

PRESERVATION: The first acquisition in the history of the American Battlefield Trust was on a Shenandoah Valley battlefield. On Oct. 12, 1988, the APCWS acquired The Coaling, an 8.55-acre tract in the heart of the Port Republic battlefield. Since then, in 58 acquisitions, the Trust has saved more than 5,700 acres on 10 Valley battlefields, including 729 acres at Cedar Creek, 1,225 acres at Cool Spring, 281 acres at Cross Keys, 424 acres at Fisher's Hill, 583 acres at McDowell, 946 acres at Port Republic and 625 acres at two of the Winchester battlefields.

This photograph, said to show Confederate prisoners after the Battle of Front Royal in May 1862, is one of the few wartime photographs taken in the Shenandoah Valley.
LIBRARY OF CONGRESS

The Battle of Cross Keys. Sunday, June 7th 1862. E Forbes—
Gen. Fremont. and Gen. Jackson

This Edwin Forbes sketch ABOVE shows the Battle of Cross Keys, Va., on June 7, 1862, a resounding Confederate victory. The Trust has saved more than 280 acres of this formerly unprotected battleground. MOLLUS COLLECTION, U.S. ARMY HERITAGE AND EDUCATION CENTER (USAHEC)

There are no known wartime photographs depicting Cross Keys but this postwar image shows a battlefield similar to what the soldiers would have seen in 1862. MOLLUS COLLECTION, U.S. ARMY HERITAGE AND EDUCATION CENTER

The South Fork of the Shenandoah River at Port Republic, seen after the war, ABOVE, separated Union forces from one another and facilitated a Confederate victory at an area called The Coaling BELOW, which has been preserved by the Trust. MOLLUS COLLECTION, USAHEC; GARRY ADELMAN

ABOVE: This historic photo shows the Hackwood House, which stood amidst the fighting of the Third Battle of Winchester on Sept. 19, 1864. The photo was taken later that fall when the area served as a U.S. cavalry camp. The Trust preserved 222 acres adjacent to the house, which was built in 1777 and still stands. MOLLUS COLLECTION, USAHEC

Cedar Creek & Belle Grove National Historical Park
Middletown, Va.
BUDDY SECOR

KENTUCKY

NOWHERE WAS THE DIVIDE between North and South more stark than the border state of Kentucky. Both President Abraham Lincoln and Confederate President Jefferson Davis were born there. In May 1861, the Union-leaning state government — hoping to avoid conflict — declared neutrality. But in September the Confederate army occupied Columbus, Kentucky, and Southern sympathizers formed an alternative state government. Union Gen. U.S. Grant responded by occupying Paducah, a strategic stronghold at the confluence of the Ohio and Tennessee Rivers. The major battles in the state occurred in 1862, with the Union army winning a decisive victory in the Battle of Mill Springs in January 1862 and losing just as decisively in the Battle of Richmond in August. Union troops also won the Battle of Munfordville in September. And with the Union victory at Perryville in October in the state's largest battle, Confederate efforts to control Kentucky came to an end.

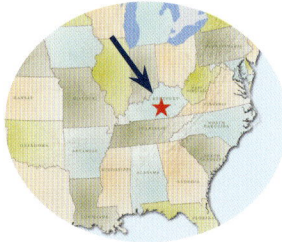

PRESERVATION: The American Battlefield Trust and its partners have preserved more than 3,000 acres at six Kentucky sites beginning in 1997, when 263 acres were saved at the Camp Wildcat battlefield. Since then, the Trust and its partners have saved more than 1,200 acres in 15 separate acquisitions at Perryville, 832 acres in 20 acquisitions at Mill Springs, 137 acres in eight transactions at Munfordville and 365 acres in four acquisitions at Richmond. The Trust also teamed with the State of Kentucky and the National Park Service to permanently preserve 380 acres at Camp Nelson, clearing the way for it to become the Camp Nelson National Monument. After the Union established a fortified base and supply depot at Camp Nelson, it became one of the largest recruitment and training centers for African-American soldiers as well as a refugee camp for their wives and children and others fleeing the war.

A school was established for the young African Americans who escaped bondage and flocked to the safety of Camp Nelson's refugee camp as the Union army liberated parts of Kentucky.
UNIVERSITY OF KENTUCKY, SPECIAL COLLECTION AND RESEARCH CENTER

ABOVE:
The Oliver Perry House, built in the mid-1850s, became the Union military headquarters at Camp Nelson during the war. LEFT: It still stands and served as a backdrop as the Trust's Kris White shot a video featuring National Park Service ranger Ernie Price.
UNIVERSITY OF KENTUCKY SPECIAL COLLECTION AND RESEARCH CENTER; GARRY ADELMAN.

LEFT:
By November 1864, refugees overwhelmed Camp Nelson. The army summarily expelled them from the camp to fend for themselves through a harsh winter. More than 100 died of exposure. The ensuing controversy prompted a reversal in policy. By the end of the war, dwellings had been constructed to house the former slaves. UNIVERSITY OF KENTUCKY, SPECIAL COLLECTION AND RESEARCH CENTER.

BELOW: African American Union soldiers stand watch on the parapet of Fort Halleck overlooking Columbus, Ky., on the Mississippi River in 1863. WES COWAN COLLECTION

The Battle of Perryville in October 1862 was the largest Civil War battle in Kentucky. This 1907 photo is one of the earliest known images of the battlefield.
UNIVERSITY OF KENTUCKY, SPECIAL COLLECTION AND RESEARCH CENTER

Perryville Battlefield State Historic Site
Perryville, Ky.
DANIEL KIRCHNER

THE WILDERNESS

VIRGINIA

GEN. U.S. GRANT'S VICTORIES in the Western Theater prompted President Lincoln to bring him East, promote him to lieutenant general and put him in command of all Union armies. Grant put Gen. William T. Sherman in charge in the Western Theater and remained with the Army of the Potomac, intent on attacking Lee in Virginia. Just after midnight on May 4, 1864, the army began the Overland Campaign, crossing the Rapidan River west of Fredericksburg. The following day, Union and Confederate corps clashed along the Orange Turnpike in an area of thick undergrowth and trees known as the Wilderness. Grant hoped to push through it quickly; Lee decided to fight there to blunt the effectiveness of federal artillery. Stalled after two days of fierce, bloody fighting in the Wilderness, often at close quarters, Grant called off his attack and pulled back, but not in retreat. Instead, he pivoted and continued toward Richmond, marching the army about 10 miles southeast to Spotsylvania Court House. The inde-cisive battle at the Wilderness led to some 30,000 casualties, with about 17,000 on the Union side and 13,000 among the Confederates. But Grant was undeterred. He had crossed the Rapidan with more than 122,000 men and an iron will to press the attack no matter what.

PRESERVATION: Since 2007, in seven acquisitions, the Trust and its partners have preserved 457 acres to supplement the land that is already part of the Wilderness unit of the Fredericksburg & Spotsylvania National Military Park. Notable among the Trust's saves at the Wilderness is 50 acres near the entrance to the national park that was slated to become a Walmart Supercenter in 2008. The Trust organized and led a coalition of local and national groups in an intense three-year political and legal fight that ended in a courtroom on the eve of a trial in January 2011 when Walmart agreed to settle and find a different location. The Trust also has saved the site of Todd's Tavern, where much fighting took place at a crucial intersection about halfway between the Wilderness and Spotsylvania battlefields.

This 1866 photo looks west up the Orange Turnpike with the ruins of the Wilderness Tavern at right. The area was the site of several Union field hospitals. The Trust has saved land on the right side of the road in the distance. AMERICAN ANTIQUARIAN SOCIETY

LEFT: In this 1866 photograph of Saunders Field, scene of some of the fiercest fighting in the Battle of the Wilderness, the white fence around the U.S. National Cemetery Number One is visible at upper right.
ABOVE: The photographer also took a closeup of the temporary cemetery. The Trust has preserved land on both the east and west sides of Saunders Field, shown BELOW in a modern photo.
AMERICAN ANTIQUARIAN SOCIETY; BUDDY SECOR

The Wilderness battlefield was extensively photographed in 1866 when the thick under-growth, dense trees and battle damage were still evident. ROBIN STANFORD COLLECTION, LIBRARY OF CONGRESS.

BELOW: Some sections of the Wilderness remain as dense as they were in 1864, including this area in the Union rear. JENNIFER GOELLNITZ

The army marching past Todds Tavern

Todd's Tavern, sketched during the war by Alfred R. Waud, ABOVE, and photographed in 1866, BELOW, was at a key intersection where cavalry clashed as the Confederates fought to slow the Union advance following the Battle of the Wilderness. The Trust has preserved more than 141 acres here, including the tavern site. LIBRARY OF CONGRESS

SPOTSYLVANIA

VIRGINIA

ON MAY 8, 1864, as Union troops neared Spotsylvania Court House, they discovered that elements of the Confederate army were already there. An initial Union assault failed and both sides began to dig in and reinforce their lines. The following day, a Union corps commander, Gen. John Sedgwick, was killed and on May 10 a massive early evening Union attack near the "Mule Shoe," a salient in the Confederate line, was repulsed. The next day saw a break in the fighting but at Yellow Tavern outside Richmond, Gen. J.E.B. Stuart was mortally wounded. May 12, one of the war's bloodiest days, brought fierce combat at Spotsylvania's "Bloody Angle" and caused almost 12,000 casualties but no resolution to the battle. Another massive Union attack on May 18 failed to break the Confederate line. By the time the fighting ended on May 21, more than 30,000 soldiers had been killed, wounded, captured or were missing, including about 18,400 bluecoats. The Confederates lost fewer men — about 12,700 — but a larger percentage of their army.

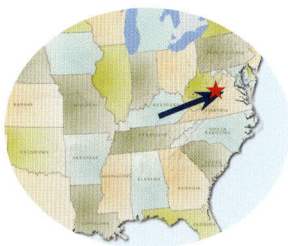

PRESERVATION: In six acquisitions at the Spotsylvania battlefield, the Trust has saved more than 153 acres, including land at the Harris Farm, near Laurel Hill and close the East Angle.

In this tight detail from a larger photo taken at Harris Farm, soldiers of the 1st Massachusetts Heavy Artillery are blurred in the multi-second camera exposure as they labor to bury the dead after the Battle of Spotsylvania. **LIBRARY OF CONGRESS**

On May 10, a fierce, concentrated but ultimately unsuccessful attack of 12 compact Union regiments (about 4,500 soldiers) under Col. Emory Upton came across the open field in the distance from right to left. Two days later a much larger attack climaxed along the works in the foreground, now comprising part of the Bloody Angle. LIBRARY OF CONGRESS

The McCoull house on the Spotsylvania battlefield, photographed in 1866, was heavily damaged during the battle but later repaired and reoccupied. ROBIN STANFORD COLLECTION, LIBRARY OF CONGRESS.

ABOVE: Photographer Timothy O'Sullivan's darkroom wagon is parked in front of "Whig Hill," the estate of tobacco farmer Francis Corbin Beverly, which became the headquarters of Union Gen. Gouverneur K. Warren during the second week of the Battle of Spotsylvania. BELOW: O'Sullivan also turned his camera around and took a view looking north from the home across the open fields, with entrenchments and the Union artillery reserve park in the distance. LIBRARY OF CONGRESS.

Spotsylvania Courthouse Battlefield
Fredericksburg & Spotsylvania National Military Park
Fredericksburg, Va.
JENNIFER GOELLNITZ

Spotsylvania Courthouse Battlefield
Fredericksburg & Spotsylvania National Military Park
Fredericksburg, Va.
JAMES SALZANO

RESACA & NEW HOPE CHURCH

GEORGIA

ON MAY 7, 1864, the day before the Battle of Spotsylvania, Union Gen. W. T. Sherman and his 99,000-man army invaded Georgia in pursuit of the Confederates. The outnumbered Confederate army, with some 60,000 men, was now under the command of Gen. Joseph E. Johnston, who had replaced Bragg. The Rebels prepared to make a stand at Rocky Face Ridge, about 15 miles from the Tennessee border. Five days of engagements led to about 1,500 casualties before Johnston fell back to Resaca, about 75 miles northwest of Atlanta. There, after another three days of indecisive fighting on May 13-15 and some 5,500 casualties, Johnston decided to withdraw when a Union force threatened his flank. Johnston established another line at Dallas, New Hope Church and Pickett's Mill, about 25 miles from Atlanta. On May 25, about 16,000 Union troops attacked a much smaller but well-entrenched Confederate force of some 4,000 and were mauled, losing more than 1,600 men while the Confederates had about 400 casualties. The Confederate victory stalled the Union advance until early June, but soon Sherman was again on the move, and Johnston was forced to move as well to prevent being flanked, pulling back closer to Atlanta.

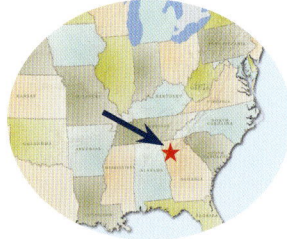

PRESERVATION: The Trust and its partners have preserved 926 acres in two acquisitions at the Rocky Face Ridge battlefield, where there is now a public park with a walking trail. And it has preserved almost five acres at New Hope Church, Dallas and Pickett's Mill.

Rocky Face Ridge Battlefield
Whitfield County, Ga.
MICHAEL BYERLEY

From May 13 to 15, 1864, Sherman's troops fought the well-entrenched Confederates under Johnston at Resaca, Georgia, in one of the major battles of the Atlanta Campaign. George Barnard took these photos of the battlefield in 1866. METROPOLITAN MUSEUM OF ART

Resaca Battlefield Historic Site
Resaca, Ga.
NOEL BENADOM

BELOW: Barnard had been with Sherman in 1864 and brought his camera back to Georgia two years later to photograph the battlefields. Despite the passage of time, the shell-splintered trees, abandoned earthworks and detritus of battle were still evident on the battlefield at New Hope Church.
METROPOLITAN MUSEUM OF ART

RIGHT: Union troops nicknamed the New Hope Church battlefield the "Hell Hole" because of the rugged terrain and the mauling they took attacking Confederate lines. METROPOLITAN MUSEUM OF ART

BELOW: The Trust has preserved 12 acres at Pine Mountain, where the armies clashed on June 14-15, 1864. Among the relatively few casualties was Confederate Gen. Leonidas Polk, cut in two by a direct hit from a Union shell. LIBRARY OF CONGRESS

NORTH ANNA
VIRGINIA

AFTER TWO WEEKS of bloody fighting at Spotsylvania, Grant concluded he was not going to break Lee's line. On May 20, 1864, he once again began moving the Army of the Potomac south and east. Lee responded in kind and established a defensive line on the south side of the North Anna River. Union troops arrived at Jericho Mill about 1:30 p.m. on May 23 and found the crossing there undefended. Two divisions crossed before the Confederates engaged the federals. Further downstream, part of the Union army crossed at Chesterfield Bridge and attacked the Confederates there on May 24. But a bend in the river kept the two Union forces separated, while Lee was able to again establish a strong, unbroken line. Two days of fighting produced another indecisive result before Grant pulled his troops back across the river and once again began marching south and west, drawing ever closer to Richmond.

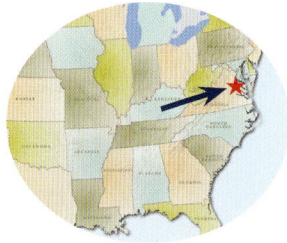

PRESERVATION: The Trust made its first acquisition at North Anna in 2014, saving the $3 million, 654-acre Anchors Down Farm. Since then, after three more acquisitions, the Trust has saved 876 acres where fighting occurred. With its Anchors Down purchase, the Trust saved nearly all of the battleground at Jericho Mill as well as the mill site and both sides of the river crossing.

Smoke rises from the wreckage of the Richmond, Fredericksburg and Potomac railroad bridge over the North Anna River in May 1864.
LIBRARY OF CONGRESS

LEFT: A group of 50th New York Engineers build a road on the south bank of the North Anna River on May 24, 1864, as the first day of the two-day Battle of North Anna rages nearby. LIBRARY OF CONGRESS

In the modern photo more than a century and a half later, Trust members and friends, supervised by President David N. Duncan, recreated the scene on a winter's day at the spot where the 1864 photo was taken. JEFF MCKINNEY

RIGHT: A group of Union soldiers bathe in the North Anna River in May 1864. In the distance is the wreckage of the railroad bridge of the Richmond, Fredericksburg and Potomac Railroad. LIBRARY OF CONGRESS

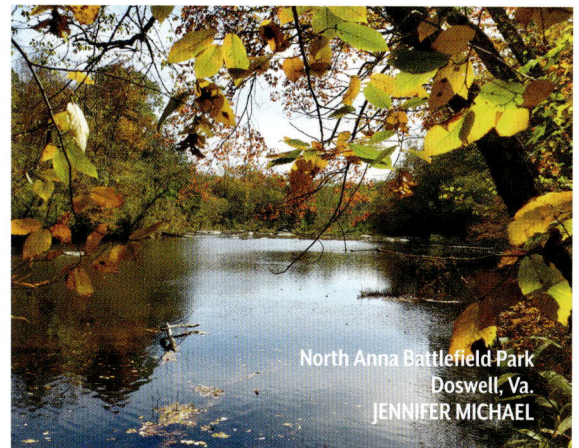

North Anna Battlefield Park
Doswell, Va.
JENNIFER MICHAEL

COLD HARBOR

VIRGINIA

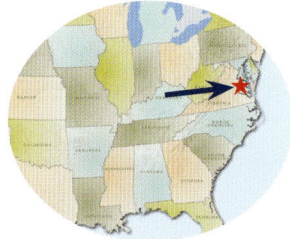

BY MAY 31, 1864, Grant's army was close to Cold Harbor, a small crossroads 10 miles northeast of Richmond. But Lee had already arrived, and his 62,000 troops were digging in and creating another strong defensive position. Fighting began on May 31 but the bloody battle is best known for Grant's disastrous frontal assault in the early morning of June 3, when portions of three infantry corps attacked along a three-mile front. In the horrific, initial fighting, nearly 7,000 Union soldiers were killed or wounded, and the toll rose as the fighting continued through the morning. At 12:30 p.m., after riding along the suffering Union line himself, Grant called off the assault. Less severe fighting continued on occasion until June 12, when Grant decided to sidestep Richmond and continue to advance south to attack Petersburg and cut off the railroad lifeline connecting Richmond to the rest of the Confederacy. Despite casualties totaling more than 12,700 men (compared to Lee's losses of about 4,600), Grant's army still had more than 100,000 men and and on June 15-16, he skillfully maneuvered this massive force across the James River on its march toward Petersburg.

PRESERVATION: When the Trust made its first save of battlefield land at Cold Harbor, only a tiny part of the battlefield was preserved as part of the Richmond National Battlefield Park. Since then, the Trust has remained an interested and active buyer, picking up tracts all along the wide battlefront as landowners decide to sell. As of mid-2024, the Trust has made 21 acquisitions totaling almost 292 acres, but hundreds more still need to be preserved.

The Cold Harbor Tavern sat at the Cold Harbor crossroads which lends its name to the battle. The Trust preserved this site, removed a modern structure and installed interpretive signs. LIBRARY OF CONGRESS

In one of the most dramatic and gruesome photographs of the Civil War, a reburial party exhumes the remains of soldiers in battlefield graves for reinterment at the nearby Cold Harbor National Cemetery.
LIBRARY OF CONGRESS

Members of the Center for Civil War Photography examine the likely location of the photo above near the Cold Harbor Visitor Center during the 2019 Image of War seminar.
LARRY KASPEREK

Union Lt. Gen. Ulysses S. Grant was photographed by famed Civil War photographer Mathew Brady at Cold Harbor in June 1864.
LIBRARY OF CONGRESS

LEFT: This photo of the Cold Harbor Battlefield from *Gardner's Sketch Book of the Civil War* likely shows land in the distance that has been preserved by the Trust. LIBRARY OF CONGRESS

BELOW:
After Cold Harbor, the seat of war moved southward to Petersburg, where photographers took numerous photos of the Union's initial attempts to capture the city. LIBRARY OF CONGRESS

KENNESAW MOUNTAIN
GEORGIA

AS GRANT AND LEE continued their bloody sashay south through Virginia, Sherman and Johnston did the same in Georgia. By June 27, Johnston's Confederates were entrenched at Kennesaw Mountain, less than 20 miles northwest of Atlanta. In the biggest battle thus far of Sherman's campaign in Georgia, thousands of Union troops launched frontal assaults up the mountain against the well-protected Confederate defenses. The Union troops got close enough that Confederates hurled rocks at them during the battle, but the gray line held and repulsed the federals by noon. The fighting resulted in 3,000 Union casualties while the Confederates lost only 1,000 men. The opposing armies remained in place for another five days until Sherman began moving again and Johnston's men evacuated their trenches and withdrew closer to Atlanta to establish a new defensive line. On July 17, Johnston was replaced by Gen. John Bell Hood, who launched attacks but failed to stop Sherman's relentless advance. The Confederates evacuated Atlanta on Sept. 1. Sherman began his destructive March to the Sea on Nov. 16 and completed it before the end of the year, handing the newly reelected President Lincoln Savannah as a Christmas present.

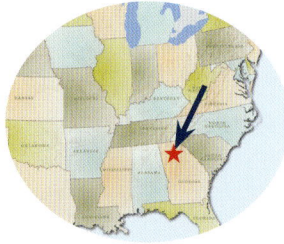

PRESERVATION: As of mid-2024, the Trust and its partners have saved 2,205 acres of land at seven Civil War battlefields in Georgia, including 3.7 acres at Kennesaw Mountain, 926 acres at Rocky Face Ridge and 1,044 acres at Resaca.

Photographer George Barnard captured a view of the Kennesaw Mountain Battlefield in 1866 from the Confederate fortifications.
METROPOLITAN MUSEUM OF ART

After Sherman's troops failed to dislodge entrenched Confederates in the Battle of Kennesaw Mountain on June 27, 1864, he shifted his army around their flank, forcing them to fall back closer to Atlanta.
METROPOLITIAN MUSEUM OF ART

Kennesaw Mountain National Battlefield Park
Kennesaw, Ga.
BRIAN KEELEY PHOTOGRAPHY

NEW MARKET HEIGHTS

VIRGINIA

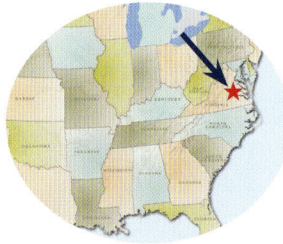

I**N SEPTEMBER 1864,** during the Siege of Petersburg, Grant moved to cut off the Southside Railroad west of the city. To put greater pressure on Lee and his shrinking army, Grant ordered attacks against the south end of the Confederate line near the James River southeast of Richmond. At dawn on September 29, Gen. Benjamin Butler's Army of the James attacked Confederate positions on the high ground above New Market Road and at nearby Fort Harrison. In the Battle of New Market Heights, also known as the Battle of Chaffin's Farm, Union troops were pushing ahead on both fronts until the Confederates rallied and prevented a breakthrough. A brigade of U. S. Colored Troops joined the fray and fought bravely, eventually pushing the Confederates back. Sixteen men were awarded the Medal of Honor for their bravery, including 14 black soldiers. Union troops also took Fort Harrison. As Grant had hoped, Lee was forced to respond. He personally lead 10,000 troops to reinforce the embattled Confederates at the cost of weakening his army at Petersburg. A Confederate counterattack on Sept. 30 was unsuccessful. Both sides established new lines and dug in. More than 25,000 Union troops fought about 14,500 Confederates in the battle, which produced almost 6,000 casualties, including 4,150 Union troops.

PRESERVATION: The Trust's first preservation effort in connection with the Battle of New Market Heights came in 2002, when it granted $45,000 to Richmond Battlefields Association to purchase 9.23 acres near Fort Harrison, which is part of the Richmond National Battlefield Park. With four acquisitions in addition to the grant, the Trust and it partners have now saved 87.5 acres of the battlefield.

This two-image panorama taken southeast of Richmond in 1864 may show the New Market Heights Battlefield, where 14 black soldiers in the Union Army were awarded the Medal of Honor for their bravery during the battle of September 29, 1864. LIBRARY OF CONGRESS; PANORAMA BY MIKE GORMAN.

After its capture, black soldiers manned the Confederate Fort Harrison. It was renamed Fort Burnham and became part of the Union line outside Richmond in 1865. This was a hostile front and enemy fortifications are visible in the middle distance along with a Confederate or two on the parapet. The fort was just a few miles north of the New Market Heights Battlefield and remains under the stewardship of the National Park Service. LIBRARY OF CONGRESS

New Market Heights Battlefield
Henrico County, Va.
NOEL KLINE

FRANKLIN & NASHVILLE

TENNESSEE

AFTER GIVING UP ATLANTA on September 1, 1864, Confederate Gen. John Bell Hood and his 33,000 soldiers marched back into Tennessee, hoping to stymie Sherman's advance by attacking the Union stronghold at Nashville. But by 1864, the Union had a huge manpower advantage. Sherman dispatched Gen. John Schofield's 30,000-man Army of the Ohio toward Nashville, where Gen. George Thomas was gathering reinforcements. After a Union victory in fighting at Spring Hill on Nov. 29, 1864, Schofield's army that night somehow managed to march directly past Hood's army and continue north toward Nashville. At Franklin, 22 miles south of Nashville, Hood caught up with Schofield's army and launched a massive late-afternoon frontal assault on Nov. 30 that was larger than Pickett's Charge. Hood suffered more than 6,200 casualties — almost 20 percent of his army — in one of the costliest Confederate attacks of the war. Schofield continued on to Nashville. Hood followed, reaching Nashville on Dec. 2, determined to continue his campaign despite now being outnumbered two to one. Hood entrenched and hoped to bait a costly Union attack. Grant and President Lincoln urged Thomas to attack, but he delayed, citing weather and other reasons. Finally, he attacked on Dec. 15 and followed it up the next day, breaking the Confederate line. Hood suffered another 6,000 casualties and pulled back to save what was left of his army. But it was so decimated, it was no longer a serious threat. The Union was now in full control of the Western Theater as Sherman finished ravaging Georgia and set his sights on South Carolina. It was now only a matter of time before the Confederacy fell.

PRESERVATION: The ongoing preservation of the Franklin battlefield is one of the great success stories of the Trust and its partners. Most of the battlefield has been built upon, but developed land is being acquired, the buildings or homes are being removed and the land is being restored to its battlefield appearance. Two historic homes — the Carter House and Carnton — have joined forces with local preservationists in the Franklin's Charge organization as acquisitions continue. In 14 transactions since 1996, the Trust and its partners have saved 181.5 acres. Eight of those acquisitions were developed parcels of less than an acre in the heart of the battlefield. South of Franklin, at Spring Hill, the Trust and its partners have saved more than 190 acres of core battlefield land. At Nashville, the Trust has preserved two key acres at Fort Negley and one acre at Shy's Hill.

Franklin Battlefield
Franklin, Tenn.
MICHAEL BYERLEY

1880s

A post-war photograph shows the Carter Cotton Gin on the Franklin battlefield, the high-water mark of the massive, unsuccessful Confederate assault on Nov. 30, 1864.
MOLLUS COLLECTION, USAHEC

2009

As the City of Franklin grew over the years, development covered much of the battlefield, if not the unpleasant memories it had for many Southerners. Near the site of the Carter cotton gin, a strip mall and a Domino's pizza covered hallowed ground along Columbia Avenue.
GARRY ADELMAN

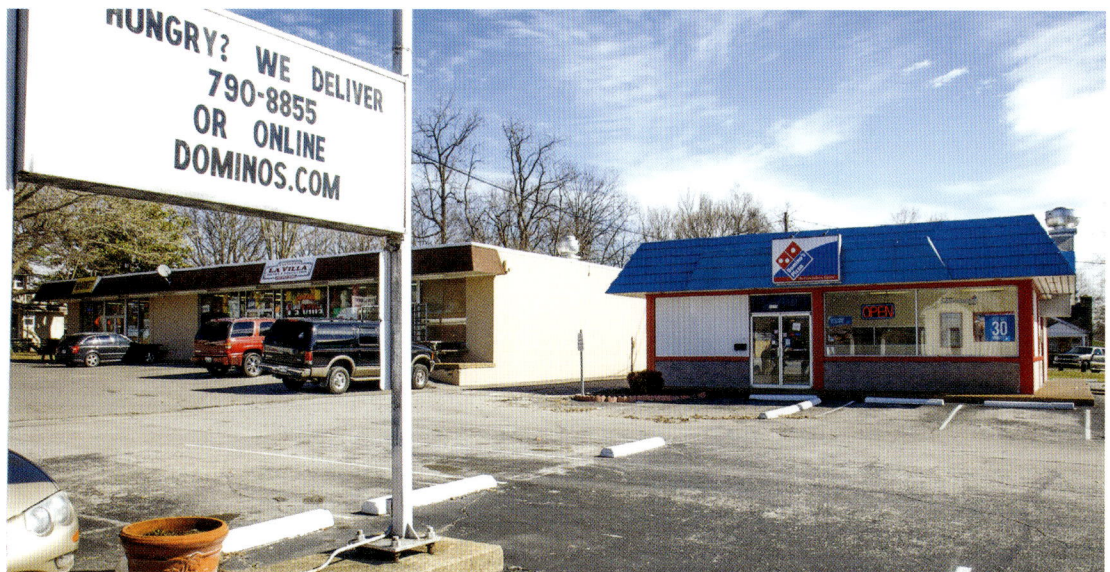

2024

In a remarkable turnaround for preservation, the Trust and its partners acquired the commercial properties, removed the modern buildings, restored the landscape to its wartime appearance and made it part of Carter Hill Park, a battlefield memorial.
GARRY ADELMAN

After the Battle of Franklin, the McGavock family donated two acres at their Carnton estate for a Confederate cemetery where almost 1,500 Southerners who died in the battle were interred. TENNESSEE STATE ARCHIVES

American Battlefield Trust members and staff on the grounds of the Carter House at its 2023 Annual Conference. BUDDY SECOR

Hundreds of tents are visible in this image of the Union outer lines at Nashville in December 1864. LIBRARY OF CONGRESS

Citizens of Nashville gather below the State Capitol on December 15 or 16, 1864, to watch for the smoke and hear the shelling in the distant Battle of Nashville in this two-plate panorama by photographer Jacob Coonley.
LIBRARY OF CONGRESS

PETERSBURG
VIRGINIA

AFTER BLOODY ASSAULTS from June 15-18, 1864, failed to break the Confederate lines at Petersburg, Grant chose to lay siege to the city. Month after month, the siege dragged on with battles at the Crater, Globe Tavern, Reams Station, Peebles Farm, Hatcher's Run, as well as occasional skirmishes and artillery duels between the entrenched armies as Grant constantly worked to stretch Lee's line. By February 1865, Lee's army had shrunken to about 45,000 soldiers to fight Grant's force of 110,000. The armies clashed at White Oak Road on March 31, 1865, and at Five Forks on April 1. The following day, Union forces launched an all-out assault and broke Lee's line south of Petersburg. Lee was forced to evacuate both Petersburg and Richmond and retreat with his diminished force. On April 3, victorious Union troops entered both Petersburg and the Confederate capital, finally achieving the primary objective of the Overland Campaign.

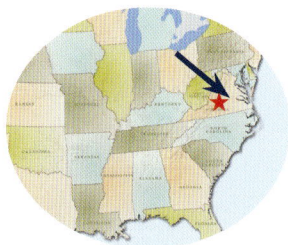

PRESERVATION: In seven acquisitions at the Breakthrough battlefield of April 2, the Trust and its partners have saved 417 acres. The Trust has also saved 130 other acres of the Petersburg battlefield as well as 388 acres at Hatcher's Run, 97 acres at Globe Tavern, 392 acres at Ream's Station, 90.5 acres at Peebles Farm, 963 acres in 14 acquisitions at White Oak Road, 419 acres at Five Forks, 11.7 acres at Boydton Plank Road and 7.9 acres at Dinwiddie Court House. That's more than 2,900 acres at 10 different battle locations connected to the siege.

This post-war photograph shows the remains of the Crater on the Petersburg battlefield.
JOHN RICHTER COLLECTION

Reams Station Battlefield
Petersburg, Va.
MATT GEORGE

Preserved land at Fort Welch, Peebles Farm/
Breakthrough Battlefield
Petersburg National Battlefield
Petersburg, Va.
CHRIS LANDON

Intact trenches.
Hatcher's Run Battlefield
Petersburg, Va.
KRISTI ANN GORDON

White Oak Road Battlefield
Dinwiddie County, Va.
KRISTI ANN GORDON

Fort Conahey was on the Union line at Petersburg near where the Breakthrough took place on April 2, 1865. The Trust and its partners have preserved the site of the fort, where earthworks are still visible. LIBRARY OF CONGRESS

The remains of two dead Confederates, one in the open and the other nearly covered in mud, lie in Confederate Fort Mahone at Petersburg after the victorious Union assault on April 2, 1865. LIBRARY OF CONGRESS.

The stacked arms of Union soldiers at Petersburg at the end of the Civil War. LIBRARY OF CONGRESS

THE FINAL DAYS
VIRGINIA / NORTH CAROLINA

AS MARCH 1865 came to an end, the major Confederate armies in Virginia and North Carolina teetered on the brink of collapse. Gen. Joseph E. Johnston's force in North Carolina had been beaten at Bentonville in mid-March and limped northward toward Raleigh. On April 2, 1865, Grant's forces finally smashed through the Confederate line at Petersburg and Lee's shrunken army fled westward, hoping to reach supply trains at Farmville. From there he hoped to march southward and link up with Johnston. But Grant hounded Lee with a dogged pursuit as the Confederate army limped westward. On April 6, the last major engagement of the war occurred at Sailor's Creek when federal troops exploited a gap in Lee's retreating columns, overwhelming and capturing a quarter of Lee's army — more than 7,700 men including six Confederate generals. On April 7, Union troops captured the valuable supplies at Farmville. The following day, at Appomattox Court House, Lee found his route blocked by Union cavalry. He had only two choices: Continue a futile fight or surrender and save the lives of his remaining men. On April 9, Lee surrendered. On April 12, Confederates surrendered Mobile, Ala., the last major city they held. President Lincoln was assassinated on April 14. And on April 26, his assassin, John Wilkes Booth, was fatally wounded upon his capture. The same day, Johnston surrendered his army and other forces to Sherman at Durham, N.C. The Civil War was over.

PRESERVATION: In 14 acquisitions dating back to 2000, the Trust and its partners have saved 512 acres at Appomattox Court House. It has also saved 1,319 acres in seven transactions at Sailor's Creek, 45 acres at Appomattox Station and 175 acres at High Bridge. And at Bentonville, N.C., where Johnston surrendered, the Trust has made more individual acquisitions than at any other location, with 61 transactions from 1990 to mid-2024 totaling almost 2,065 acres.

Bentonville Battlefield State Historic Site
Four Oaks, N.C.
DAVID DAVIS

Confederate Gen. Robert E. Lee surrendered his army to Union Gen. U.S. Grant here at the McLean House at Appomattox Court House on April 9, 1865. This photo was taken soon after. LIBRARY OF CONGRESS

Appomattox Court House National Historical Park
Appomattox, Va.
SHENANDOAH SANCHEZ

This circa 1904 photo shows the remains of Bennett Place, the farm home of James Bennett near Durham, N.C., where Confederate Gen. Joseph E. Johnston surrendered the last remaining Confederate army to Union Gen. William T. Sherman on April 26, 1865. LIBRARY OF CONGRESS.

THIS BATTLEFIELD DOESN'T EXIST ANYMORE.

Yellow Tavern Battlefield
Henrico County, Va.
JAMIE BETTS PHOTO

BUT YOU CAN HELP SAVE OTHERS BEFORE THEY'RE LOST.

THE AMERICAN BATTLEFIELD TRUST preserves America's hallowed battlegrounds and educates the public about what happened there and why it matters. Every day, dozens of hallowed battlefield acres are lost to development around the country. We see battlefields as outdoor classrooms, teaching young and old alike about the sacrifices made during our nation's turbulent first century to secure the freedoms that all Americans enjoy today. These were places where crucial chapters of the American story were written. Where ordinary citizens – farmers, merchants and laborers – displayed extraordinary valor fighting for independence and freedom.

Join now and you'll receive our award-winning magazine *Hallowed Ground* free along with access to one of the most extensive history websites and social media apps covering the American Revolution, War of 1812 and the Civil War.

Learn more about our mission and how you can help at ***www.battlefields.org***

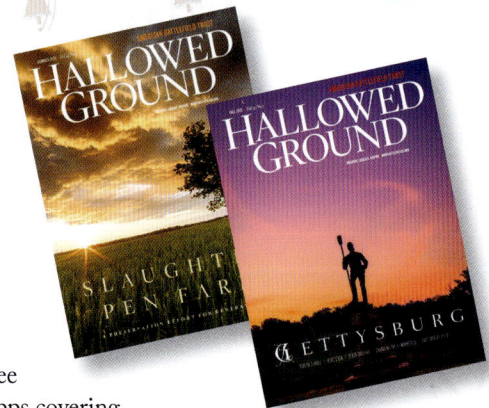

AMERICAN BATTLEFIELD TRUST ★ ★ ★

PRESERVE. EDUCATE. INSPIRE.